My name is

_____.

Will you please read to me?
Thank you.

ZONDERKIDZ

The Beginner's Bible®
Copyright © 2005 by Zondervan
Illustrations © 2005, 2016 by Zondervan

Requests for information should be addressed to:
Zondervan, 3900 *Sparks Dr. SE, Grand Rapids, Michigan 49546*

This edition: ISBN 978-0-310-75013-0

Library of Congress Cataloging-in-Publication Data

The beginner's Bible: timeless children's stories—Rev. ed.-
     p. cm.
     "Copyright, Zondervan"—T.p. verso.
     Included index.
     ISBN 0-310-70962-8 (hardcover)
     1. Bible stories, English   I. Zondervan.
BS551.3.D48 2005
220.9'505 — dc22   2004026266

Illustrations: Denis Alonso
Editor: Catherine DeVries
Editorial assistance: Kristen Tuinstra
Theological review: Michael J. Klassen, M.Div., Fuller Theological Seminary
Art Direction and Design: Jody Langley

Printed in Italy

21 22 23 /RTLO/ 20 19

The Beginner's Bible ®

Timeless Children's Stories

ZONDERkidz

Contents

OLD TESTAMENT

NEW TESTAMENT

The Old Testament

Timeless Bible Stories

The Beginning

Genesis 1

In the beginning, the world was empty.
Darkness was everywhere.
But God had a plan.

God separated the light from the darkness.
"Let there be light!" he said.
And the light turned on.
He called the light "day."
And he called the darkness "night."
This was the end of the very first day.

Then God said, "I will divide the waters."
He separated the waters in the clouds
above from the waters in the ocean below.
He called the space between them "sky."
This was the end of the second day.

Next, God rolled back the waters
and some dry ground appeared.
He made plants of many shapes and colors.
He made mountains, hills, and valleys.
This was the end of the third day.

God put a shining sun in
the sky for daytime.
He put a glowing moon and twinkling
stars in the sky for nighttime.
This was the end of the fourth day.

On the fifth day,
God made swishy fish and
squiggly creatures to live in the ocean.
Then God made birds
to fly across the sky.

On the sixth day, God made animals
to creep, crawl, hop, and gallop.
Then from the dust, God made the most
wonderful creature of all—a person.
God named him Adam.
On the seventh day, God rested.

Adam and Eve

Genesis 2

God had planted a beautiful garden for
Adam in a place called Eden.
A river flowed through the garden.

Adam loved his new home.
His job was to name all the animals
and care for the garden.
Adam loved all the animals,
but he could not find a friend
that was just right for him.
So God created a woman.

Adam named her Eve.
She was just right for Adam.
Adam and Eve loved each other.
Together they took care
of God's garden.

The Sneaky Snake

Genesis 3

Many trees grew in the Garden of Eden.
God told Adam and Eve, "You may eat
the fruit from any tree except for one.
Never eat the fruit from the tree
of the knowledge of good and evil."

Now, there was a sneaky snake
in the garden.
One day, the snake saw Eve
near the special tree.
It hissed, "Did God *really* tell you
not to eat the fruit from this tree?"

The snake wanted Eve to disobey God.
It said, "You should try some
of this tasty fruit.
If you eat it, you will be like God.
You will be able to tell the difference
between good and evil."

The fruit looked tasty.
Eve remembered what God had said,
but she ate the fruit anyway.
Then Eve gave some to Adam.
He took a bite too.

As the sun was going down,
Adam and Eve heard God
walking through the garden.
He was looking for them.
Adam and Eve hid among the trees.
They were afraid.

"What have you done?" God asked.
"Did you eat the fruit from
the forbidden tree?"
Adam said, "Yes, but Eve gave it to me."
Eve said, "Yes, but the snake tricked me."

God told the snake, "Because of what you did, you will always crawl on your belly." Then he told Adam and Eve, "Because you disobeyed me, you can no longer live in the garden."

Adam and Eve left the garden.
God placed angels and a flaming sword
to guard the entrance.
Adam and Eve would not be allowed
in the garden again.

Noah's Ark

Genesis 6–9

After Adam and Eve left the garden,
many people were born.
The people kept doing bad things,
and they forgot about God.

Except Noah. Noah loved God.

God was sad that everyone but Noah
forgot about him.
He told Noah about his plan to start over.
"Make yourself an ark," God said.
"Here's how." So Noah and his family
began working on the ark.

When it was done, God said,
"Take your family and two of
every animal into the ark."
Animals creeped, crawled, hopped,
and galloped onto Noah's new boat.

After everyone was inside,
the rain began to fall.
And fall. And fall.
The ark rocked this way and
that way on the rising water.

Finally, the rain stopped.
Water covered everything!
Everyone inside the ark was safe.
Noah and his family were very happy.

One day, Noah sent a dove to find land.
It flew and flew but never found any.
So it came back. One week later,
Noah sent the dove out again.
This time it brought him an olive leaf.
Noah cheered, "It must have found land!"

The ark finally came to rest on
the top of a mountain.
God told Noah to leave the ark.
Noah and his family praised God.
God put a beautiful rainbow in the sky.
It was a sign of his promise to
never flood the whole earth again.

The Tall Tower

Genesis 11

After the flood, everyone spoke
the same language.
One word meant "hello."
One word meant "Mom,"
and one word meant "Dad."

The people said, "If we work together,
we can do anything.
Let's build a tower that goes all
the way up to heaven.
Then everyone will see
how great we are!"

The people worked on their tower.
They built it taller and taller.
They began to brag.
God did not like the way
they were acting.
It was as if they no longer needed him.

So God mixed up their language.
When they tried to talk to each other,
it sounded like "babble."
Everyone was confused!

Then God scattered the people
all over the earth.
They had to stop building their tower.
From then on, the tower
was called "Babel."

A New Home

Genesis 12–17

Abraham loved God.
So did his wife Sarah.

One day, God told Abraham
to move to a new land.
So, along with their helpers,
Abraham and Sarah packed up
and went.

Abraham's nephew was Lot.
Lot and all his helpers
went with them too.

The helpers began to fight.
There was not enough grass
for all the animals.
So Abraham said to Lot,
"You pick your own land to live on."

Lot chose the best land.
It had the most green grass
and the most water for his animals.
Lot moved to his new home.

Then God gave Abraham a blessing.
God said, "All the land you see here
will be yours forever. Also, you
and Sarah will be blessed
with many children."

God led Abraham and Sarah
to a place called Hebron.
It was beautiful.

The Visitors

Genesis 18; 21

One hot day, Abraham was resting
near his tent. He heard footsteps.

Three men were standing nearby.
Abraham went out to greet them.
"Would you like to rest in the shade?
We have plenty of cool water to drink.
Can I get you something to eat?"

Abraham told Sarah about the visitors.
He asked her to make a tasty meal.

While they were eating,
the three visitors shared some
exciting news. They said,
"Your wife is going to have a son."

49

Sarah heard what they said.
She laughed, thinking, *I am too old*.
God asked Abraham,
"Why did Sarah laugh?
Anything is possible with the LORD."

Sure enough, the next year,
Sarah had a baby boy.
They named him Isaac.

A Bride for Isaac

Genesis 24–25

When Isaac grew up, his father,
Abraham, wanted him to get married.
Abraham told one of his servants,
"Go to my homeland. There you will find
the perfect bride for Isaac."

So Abraham sent the servant
on his way with ten camels and
a lot of jewelry and clothes.
They were gifts for Isaac's new bride.

The servant reached Abraham's homeland.
He stopped by a well and prayed,
"Dear God, please show me the woman
you have chosen for Isaac.
I will know she is the one if she offers
water to me and my camels."

Before he finished praying, a young
woman with a jar walked toward the well.
After she filled her jar, the servant asked
her for a drink. She gave him a drink.
Then she gave water to his camels.
She was the answer to his prayer!
Her name was Rebekah.

The servant gave her the gifts,
and they went to meet her father.
The servant asked for his permission
to take Rebekah to Isaac.
Rebekah told the servant she
would be happy to go.

When Isaac saw Rebekah,
he fell in love with her.
Soon, they got married.
Isaac and Rebekah had twin boys
named Esau and Jacob.

Isaac's Blessing

Genesis 27

When Isaac was an old man,
he could not see very well.
He called for his firstborn son, Esau.
"Bring me my favorite dinner.
Then I will give you God's blessing."

"I will make a special meal
for you," said Esau.
Then he hunted for some meat to cook.

Isaac's wife Rebekah wanted
Jacob to get God's blessing.
So, while Esau was hunting,
she told Jacob her plan.
She made Isaac's dinner.
Then she tied goatskins
around Jacob's arms.

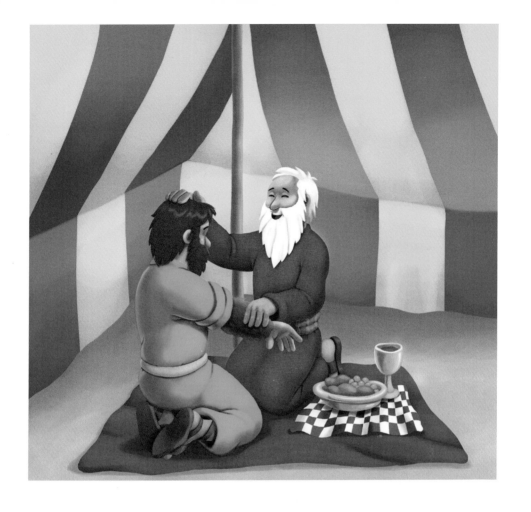

Jacob took the meal to his father.
After dinner, Isaac reached out
to bless his son.
Isaac thought Jacob was Esau.
So he gave Jacob his blessing.

When Esau returned,
he found out what had happened.
Esau was very angry.
He wanted to hurt Jacob.
Rebekah asked Isaac to send Jacob
to his uncle Laban's house.

Jacob's Dream

Genesis 28

Jacob traveled for many miles.
His uncle Laban lived far away.
One night, he lay on the ground,
using a stone for his pillow.
Jacob fell fast asleep.

Jacob dreamed of a stairway to heaven.
Angels walked up and down.
God said, "I am watching over you,
Jacob. Someday, all of this land
will belong to you and your family."

The next morning, when Jacob woke up,
he said, "The LORD is in this place!"
He took his stone pillow and set it
up as a reminder of his dream.
Jacob praised God.
Then he continued on his way.

Jacob and Esau Meet Again

Genesis 29

While Jacob lived with his uncle Laban,
he became a shepherd.
He fell in love and got married.

God blessed Jacob with many sons.
Jacob also had many sheep,
donkeys, and camels.
One day, God told Jacob to
go back to his homeland.

Jacob wanted to go back,
but he was afraid of his brother, Esau.
He thought Esau would still be
angry with him.

But Jacob obeyed God.
He and his family packed up
everything they owned.
Jacob sent servants ahead
to offer gifts to Esau.

Much to Jacob's surprise,
Esau ran to meet him.
And he gave Jacob a big hug.
They were so happy
to see each other again.

Joseph's Colorful Robe

Genesis 37

Joseph was one of Jacob's twelve sons.
Jacob loved him more than
all of his other sons.

Jacob made Joseph a colorful robe.
His brothers were jealous.
They wanted nice robes too.
And they wanted to be loved
as much as Joseph was loved.

Joseph had a dream. He told his family,
"We were bundling grain from the field.
Your bundles of grain bowed
down to mine."

Then Joseph had another dream.
He said, "This time, the sun and moon and
eleven stars were bowing down to me."
His father asked, "Does this mean our
family will bow down to you someday?"

The brothers were even more angry.
They threw Joseph into a dry well.

Along came some traders.
The brothers sold Joseph
to them as a slave.

They lied to their father and said
Joseph had been killed by a wild animal.
But God was with Joseph.

Pharaoh's Dreams

Genesis 39–41

The traders took Joseph to Egypt.
He was thrown into jail.
But he did nothing wrong.
Joseph trusted God to help him.
He made friends with some
of the prisoners.

One of them had been
a wine taster for Pharaoh.
Pharaoh was the leader of Egypt.
The wine taster said, "Last night,
I had a dream. I was picking grapes and
squeezing them into Pharaoh's cup.
Then I put the cup in his hand.
What does this mean, Joseph?"

Joseph answered, "You will be Pharaoh's
wine taster again. Once you are free,
please don't forget about me.
Help me get out of jail too."

A few days later, the wine taster's
dream came true.
He got out of jail and became
Pharaoh's wine taster once again.
But he forgot about Joseph.

Later, Pharaoh had two strange dreams.
In one dream, he saw seven heavy cows
and seven skinny cows. The skinny cows
ate up all the heavy cows.

In another dream, Pharaoh saw
seven healthy plants.
Then he saw seven dried-up plants.
The dried-up plants
ate all the healthy plants.
Pharaoh was confused.

Pharaoh's wise men were confused too.
Then the wine taster remembered Joseph.
He told Pharaoh that Joseph could
explain his dreams.
With God's help, Joseph told Pharaoh
what his dreams meant.

"For the next seven years, plenty of food
will grow. For seven years after that,
not enough food will grow because there
will be no rain." Pharaoh said,
"Joseph, you are a very wise man.
I will make you a ruler over Egypt."

Joseph Saves His Family

Genesis 42–46

For the first seven years, Joseph
was in charge of gathering extra
food for the people of Egypt.
That way, when hardly any crops grew,
there would still be plenty to eat.

The seven bad years began, and people
in other countries had no food at all.
Even Joseph's family did not have enough
to eat. So Joseph's father sent his sons
to Egypt to buy some food.

When the brothers arrived in Egypt, they
went to Joseph and bowed down to him.
They did not know he was their brother.
But Joseph knew.
Joseph sold them some food.
Then the brothers left to go home.

Sometime later, they returned to buy
more food. Just as Joseph had dreamed,
they bowed down to him—again.
Finally, Joseph told them,
"I am your brother!"
His brothers were afraid!

But Joseph told them not to be afraid.
"God meant it for good.
He had a special plan for me," he said.
They all hugged.

Joseph's brothers rushed home.
They told their father what had happened.
Jacob was so happy to hear
that Joseph was alive.
The whole family moved to Egypt.

A Baby in a Basket

Exodus 1–2:10

Many years passed. A new pharaoh ruled over Egypt. He did not know about the good things Joseph had done.

By now there were many people in Jacob's family. They were called *Israelites*.

Pharaoh did not like the Israelites.
He made them work hard.
One day, Pharaoh decided to get rid
of all the Israelite baby boys.

A woman named Jochebed had a baby
boy. She wanted to save him.
So she gently laid her baby inside a basket
and placed him in the river.
The baby started to cry.

Pharaoh's daughter saw the basket
and opened it.
She gently picked up the baby and
hugged him. "I want to keep you,"
the princess whispered.
She named him Moses because
she pulled him out of the water.

Miriam, the baby's big sister,
had been watching nearby.
She said to the princess, "I know a woman
who can help you take care of the baby."
So Miriam ran to get her mother.
Jochebed was so happy!

When Moses was a young boy,
Jochebed returned him to the princess.
He grew up in the palace.

The Burning Bush

Exodus 3

When Moses was a man,
he left the palace.
Pharaoh was still being mean
to the Israelites.
Moses tried to protect them,
so Pharaoh tried to kill Moses.

Moses escaped from Egypt.
He went to a place called Midian
and became a shepherd.

One day, while Moses was watching
his sheep, he saw something strange.
A bush was on fire, but it wasn't
burning up. From inside the bush,
God spoke, "Moses, bring my
people out of Egypt. Take them
to a new land that I will show you.
This new land is called Canaan."

Moses was worried that Pharaoh
would not listen. God told Moses
to throw his staff on the ground.
When he did, the staff became a snake!
God told Moses to reach down and grab
the snake. It became a staff again!
God said, "I will use signs like this
to show Pharaoh I have sent you."

"But I cannot speak very well,"
complained Moses.
God said, "Do not worry.
Your brother Aaron is a good speaker.
I will send him with you."

So Moses returned with Aaron to Egypt.
When they arrived, Moses told the
Israelites what God had said.

Ten Plagues

Exodus 7–12

Moses and Aaron went to
Pharaoh's palace. They said,
"You must let the Israelites go free.
If you do not, God will punish you."

Pharaoh said, "No! I do not
know your God!"
Then he made the Israelites
work even harder.

God was not pleased.

So he changed the main river to blood.

Pharaoh did not care. "I will never let the Israelites go," he said.

Then God sent frogs to Egypt.
They were sitting in chairs, hopping up
stairs, and jumping all over the beds.
Pharaoh said, "Take the frogs away, and
I will let your people go."
So God took the frogs away.

But Pharaoh changed his mind
and said, "No."
God sent more plagues on Egypt.
First were the pesky gnats.
Then came a frenzy of flies.
Next, all the animals got sick.
Then the Egyptians' skin broke
out in sores.

Damaging hailstorms came,
and then swarms of locusts ate the crops.
Then darkness covered everything.
Sometimes Pharaoh said he would
let the people go.
But after God took away each plague,
Pharaoh changed his mind and said, "No."

Moses had one last message from God
for Pharaoh: "If you do not let my
people go, the firstborn son in each
Egyptian family will die."
Pharaoh refused to listen.
So God kept his promise.
Pharaoh finally said, "Go now!"

The Red Sea

Exodus 14

Moses led the Israelites out of Egypt.
During the day, God went ahead of them
in a pillar of cloud. During the night,
God went ahead of them in a pillar of fire.

111

God led the Israelites to the
edge of the Red Sea.
Pharaoh and his army were close behind.
The Israelites did not know what to do.

They screamed, "We are trapped!
What have you done to us, Moses?"
Moses said, "Do not be afraid.
God will protect us." God's cloud came
between the Israelites and Pharaoh's army.
They could not see anything!

God told Moses, "Raise your staff
over the sea." Then the Lord pushed
back the sea to make a path.
Moses and the Israelites followed the path
through the sea and to the other side.
But Pharaoh's army followed close behind.

Moses raised his staff again, and
the sea swept away Pharaoh and his army.
Moses and all the Israelites sang praises
to God. They were free!
They weren't slaves anymore!

Food From Heaven

Exodus 16

The Israelites traveled for many days.
They were tired and hungry.
They complained to Moses,
"There is nothing to eat in the desert.
At least we had food in Egypt!
Now we are starving!"

God heard them. That evening,
God sent birds called *quail* for the
Israelites to eat.

The next morning, God sent
bread from heaven. It was called
manna and tasted like honey.
The Israelites found the manna
on the ground.
But they complained again:
"We are thirsty!"

Moses asked God what to do. God said,
"Hit the rock with your staff."
When Moses hit it, cool, fresh water
gushed out for everyone to drink.
While they were in the desert,
the Israelites would not go hungry
or thirsty again.

Ten Commandments

Exodus 19–20

God led the Israelites to a mountain.
Thunder roared and lightning flashed.
The people heard a loud trumpet blast.

Then God called Moses to the top of the
mountain and said, "I am the LORD
your God who brought you out of Egypt."
God wrote the Ten Commandments on
two stone tablets for all his people to obey.

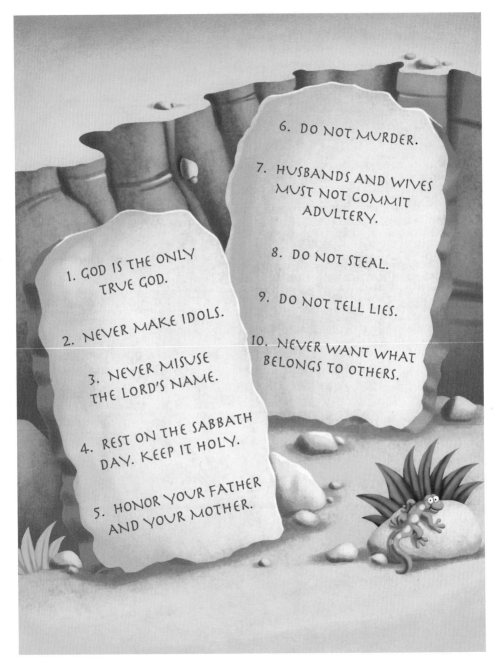

The Israelites needed a place
to worship. God showed them
exactly how to build a special tent.
It was called a *tabernacle*.
God placed a cloud over the tent.
Whenever the cloud moved,
the Israelites packed up and followed it.

Twelve Spies

Numbers 13

Finally, the Israelites arrived near the
promised land. God told Moses to send
spies there. Moses picked 12 men.
He told them, "Find out what the
people are like. See if the land is good."

The spies returned and said,
"The land is beautiful.
It is filled with plenty of food!
But the people there are big and strong!"

Joshua and Caleb said, "Do not worry.
God has promised us this land.
He will give it to us."

The rest of the Israelites did not
agree with Joshua and Caleb.
Then God said to Moses,
"The people do not have faith in me.
They cannot enter the land."
So for the next 40 years,
God's people wandered in the desert.

Joshua and the Spies

Joshua 2

After Moses died, Joshua became
the leader of the Israelites.
God led them into the promised land.
He led them to a city called Jericho.
The city was protected by high walls.

Still, two spies found a way into
the city. They went to Rahab's house.
The king of Jericho ordered his
soldiers to capture the men.

Rahab hid the men on her roof.
When the soldiers arrived, she said,
"The spies have already gone.
If you hurry, you may catch them."
So the soldiers ran off to find them.

"Thank you for helping us," the spies
told her. "When we come back,
we promise to save you and your family."
Then Rahab helped the spies escape.

The Battle of Jericho

Joshua 6

After the spies were safely home,
God told Joshua,
"March your army around Jericho
with the *priests* blowing their horns.
Do this once a day for six days.

132

"On the seventh day, have your army
march around the city seven times."
Joshua did exactly as God said.

The priests blew their trumpets.
The soldiers shouted as loud as they could.
Then the great walls of Jericho
came tumbling down!

The Israelite army rushed in
and took over the city.
The spies kept their promise to Rahab.
Her whole family was saved!

Deborah Leads the Way

Judges 4

The Israelites lived in the
promised land for many years.
But they forgot about God.
A bad king from another land
ruled over them.
The Israelites asked God for help.

God sent them a judge named Deborah.
She loved God very much.
God gave her a plan to defeat the bad
king. She sent for a man named Barak
and told him, "God wants you to take
10,000 soldiers and wait on the hill."

The Israelites were not as
strong as their enemies.
Barak begged Deborah to go with them.
She was a strong leader. She agreed.

When the Israelites met face-to-face
with the king's army, Deborah exclaimed,
"Go! Attack them now! God is with us!"
The Israelites obeyed and won the battle.

Gideon's Battle

Judges 6–7

God's people kept disobeying his rules.
So God allowed their enemies to take all
their food away. Again, the Israelites
turned to God for help.
Again, God answered their prayers.

God chose a man named Gideon
to help his people.
God sent an angel to Gideon.
"You are a mighty warrior," said the
angel. "You will save God's people."
Gideon said, "But I'm from a family
that isn't rich or important."

Then Gideon prayed to God. "I need a
sign from you. I will put some wool
on the floor. Tomorrow, if the wool is wet
and the ground is dry, I will believe you."
The next morning, the wool was wet
and the ground was dry.

But Gideon wanted another sign.
He said to God, "Now if the wool is *dry*
and the ground is *wet*, I will be sure you
have chosen me." The next morning, God
made the wool dry and the ground wet.
Now Gideon was sure. He said,
"God, I will do whatever you say."

Over 30,000 men wanted to join Gideon's
army. "That is too many," God said.
He showed Gideon how to win
with only 300 men!
The plan sounded strange,
but Gideon trusted God.

During the night, Gideon and his men
surrounded the enemy camp.
They blew trumpets and smashed clay jars.
They waved burning torches in the air.
Their enemies were frightened.
This must be a huge army! they thought.
So they ran away. God's people won!

Samson

Judges 13; 16

The Israelites were in trouble again.
Along came a very strong man
named Samson. God had chosen
him to save the Israelites from
their enemies, the Philistines.

Samson knew that as long as
he did not cut his hair,
he would always be very strong.

Samson was in love with Delilah.
The Philistines told Delilah they
would pay her if she found out
what made Samson so strong.
At first, Samson lied to her.

"If you tie me up with ropes,"
Samson said, "I will lose my strength."
That night while Samson slept,
Delilah tied him up. Then she shouted,
"The Philistines are coming!"
Samson jumped up and broke the ropes.
Delilah kissed him and asked,
"Won't you tell me your secret?"

Samson gave in and told her,
"My strength is in my long hair."
When Samson was asleep,
Delilah had all his hair cut off.
Samson's strength was gone!
The Philistines grabbed him
and put him in jail.

A while later, the Philistines were having a big party. They brought Samson in and made fun of him.

Samson prayed to God to make him strong one last time. God did.

Samson pushed the pillars with all his might. The temple came crashing down, and Samson defeated the Philistines.

Ruth and Naomi

Ruth 1–4

Naomi grew up in the promised land,
which was also called Israel.
But now she lived far away.
She had a husband and two sons.
Ruth was married to one of the sons.
Then something sad happened.
Naomi's husband and sons died.
Not long after that, Naomi decided
to go back to her homeland.

Naomi told Ruth to return to her parents,
but Ruth did not want to leave her.
She loved Naomi so much.
"I will go wherever you go," Ruth said.
"Your home will be my home.
Your God will be my God."
So Ruth went with Naomi to Israel.

They needed food to eat. So each day,
Ruth gathered leftover grain from the
fields. A good man named Boaz owned
the land. One day, he saw Ruth in the
field. He wanted to help her. So he
left extra grain for Ruth to gather.

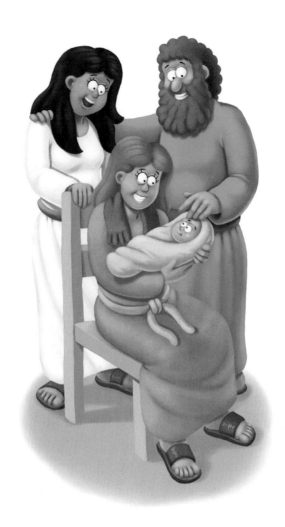

Boaz fell in love with Ruth. They got
married and had a baby boy named Obed.
God had blessed Ruth and Grandma
Naomi with a brand-new family.

Hannah's Prayer

1 Samuel 1:1–20

Hannah loved God. She wanted to have a baby, but she wasn't able to have any children.

Hannah and her husband went
to the tabernacle. She prayed to God,
"If you will give me a baby boy,
I will see that he serves you all his life."

Eli was a priest. He saw Hannah praying.
She explained, "I am crying out to the
Lord because I want him to answer
my prayer." Eli gently told her,
"Go in peace—and may God give
you what you ask for."

Sure enough, Hannah and her
husband had a baby boy.
They thanked God for their new son.
They named him Samuel.

A Voice in the Night

1 Samuel 3

When Samuel was a little boy, Hannah
brought him to live at the tabernacle.
She had promised God that Samuel
would serve him all his life. The
priest Eli would now take care of Samuel.
He would teach Samuel about God.

One night while Samuel was sleeping,
he heard a voice say, "Samuel!"
He ran to Eli and said, "Here I am."
But Eli said, "I did not call you."
Then Samuel went back to bed.

Samuel heard a voice call his
name two more times.
Each time, Samuel ran to Eli.
Finally, Eli told Samuel, "I think God
is speaking to you. Next time, say,
'Yes, LORD, I am listening.'"
Then Samuel went back to bed.

"Samuel! Samuel!" the voice said again. This time, Samuel answered, "Yes, LORD, I am listening." From that moment on, Samuel gave messages to God's people. He was a special prophet of God.

Israel's First King

1 Samuel 8–10

When Samuel was an old man,
God's people said,
"We want a king to rule over us."
Samuel asked God for help.
God told Samuel to warn the people
about all the trouble a king could bring.

A king would make the young men
join his army, and the people would
have to give the best things they
owned to support the king.
Samuel warned the people,
but they still would not listen.
Then God told Samuel to give them a king.

God led Samuel to a man named Saul.
Samuel poured oil on Saul's head.
This was a sign that Saul was God's
choice for their new king.
Saul hid because he was shy.

The people found him. Then
Samuel said, "Here is your king."
Everyone cheered and shouted,
"Long live the king!"

A Good Heart

1 Samuel 15:1–16:13

Saul was a good king for about 20 years. Then he began to disobey God. God was sorry he made Saul the king. Samuel was sad about it too.

God sent Samuel to a man named
Jesse to find a new king.
When Samuel met Jesse, he said,
"I would like to meet your sons."

When Samuel saw them, he thought,
These are strong-looking men.
God said, "I do not look at the
outside of a person. I look at the inside
of a person. I look at the heart."

170

Samuel asked Jesse,
"Do you have another son?"
Jesse said, "Yes. His name is David.
He is out in the field with the sheep."
Samuel asked to see him.

As soon as David arrived,
God told Samuel, "He is the one
I want to be the next king."
Samuel *anointed* David. He poured
oil on David's head, and David
was filled with God's power.

David and Goliath

1 Samuel 17:1–51

The Philistines were enemies of God.
Their army came to fight King Saul's army.
A giant soldier named Goliath yelled,
"Bring out your best soldier to fight me!"

"If your strongest soldier defeats me,
we will be your slaves!" he boomed.
"If I defeat him, you will be our slaves!"
King Saul's soldiers were afraid.
They did not want to fight the giant.

Meanwhile, young David was taking
food to his brothers. They were
soldiers in King Saul's army.
When David reached the camp,
he saw Goliath.
David heard the giant's challenge.

"I am not afraid to fight the giant,"
said David. King Saul called for
David and told him, "You cannot fight
the giant. You are too young."
David replied, "God will be with me."

King Saul gave his *armor* to David,
but it was big and heavy.
David wasn't used to wearing armor.

David went to a nearby stream
and picked up five stones.
He stood before Goliath.
The giant laughed at him, but
David didn't care. He said,
"I come before you in the name
of the LORD who rules over all."

David put a stone in his sling
and ran toward the giant.
Then he let the stone fly.

It hit Goliath's forehead,
and he fell to the ground!
The Philistines saw that their hero
was dead. They ran away.

Best Friends

1 Samuel 16:14–23; 18–20

King Saul became grumpy.
His servants asked David to play his harp
for the king. The music cheered him up,
so the king invited David to live in
the palace.

David became friends with
King Saul's son, Prince Jonathan,
and Jonathan's sister, Michal.

David won many battles for the king.
The people said David was a better
fighter than the king. This made King
Saul very angry and jealous. *Everyone
likes David more than me*, he thought.

King Saul became so angry that
he threw a spear at David,
but David escaped.

Then one day, Prince Jonathan warned
David, "You must run far away."
They promised to always be best friends.

King David

2 Samuel 1:1–2:4; 1 Kings 2:1–3

Saul chased David, but he never
caught him. God watched over David.
Then one day, David heard some sad news.
King Saul and Prince Jonathan
had died in battle.

The people remembered what God had
told them, and they went to find David.
"David, you are now our king!"
they exclaimed.

King David ruled over Israel for
40 years. He wrote many songs about
God, called *psalms*. He even had plans
to build a temple for God.
David was a man who was dear
to God's heart.

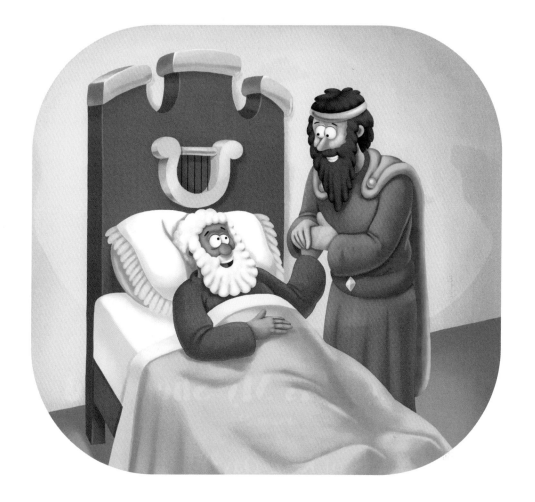

When King David was old, he told
his son Solomon, "You will be
the next king of Israel. Be strong
and obey God with all your heart.
Then he will bless you."

The Lord Is My Shepherd

Psalm 23

This is one of King David's songs
about God:
The Lord is my shepherd.
He gives me everything I need.
He lets me lie down in fields of green
grass. He leads me beside quiet waters.
He gives me new strength.

He guides me in the right paths
for the honor of his name.
Even though I walk through the
darkest valley, I will not be afraid.
You, God, are with me. Your
shepherd's rod and staff comfort me.

You prepare a feast for me
right in front of my enemies.
You pour oil on my head.
My cup runs over.

I am sure that your goodness
and love will follow me
all the days of my life.
And I will live in the house
of the LORD forever.

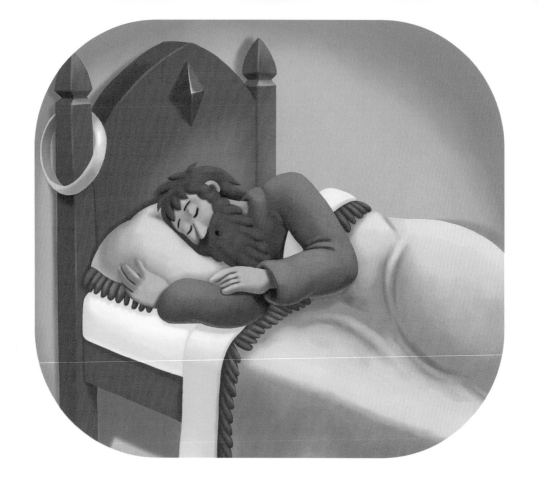

The Wise King

1 Kings 3:5–10:13

King Solomon loved God very much.
God spoke to him in a dream.
"Ask for anything you want," God said.

King Solomon answered,
"Give me wisdom so that I will know
the difference between right and wrong."
God was pleased with Solomon's answer.
"I will give wisdom to you," God said.
"I will also give you riches and honor."

King Solomon was wiser than any
other person. He spoke 3,000 *proverbs*,
or wise sayings, and wrote over 1,000
songs. He knew many things about
plants and animals.

King Solomon was famous. People
from all over the world came to see him.
The queen of Sheba came from
far away to ask him questions.

King Solomon answered all of her
questions. Then the queen said,
"You truly are a wise king.
May the Lord your God be praised!"

King Solomon ordered thousands
of workers to build a temple for God.
When the temple was finished,
it was beautiful!
King Solomon planned a celebration.

All the people of Israel came
to see the temple. They were happy
to have a new place to worship.
They all said, "God is good.
His love lasts forever!"

God Watches Over Elijah

1 Kings 16:29–17:7

After Solomon, many other kings ruled over Israel. One king was named Ahab. He did not love God.
King Ahab worshiped idols.

God had a prophet named Elijah.
God gave Elijah special messages
to tell the people.

Elijah told King Ahab, "God is angry
with you because you do not serve him."

Then Elijah told the king,
"It will not rain for a very long time.
The crops will dry up, and
your people will go hungry."
King Ahab was very angry with Elijah.

God told Elijah to escape to the desert.
He led Elijah to a brook. Each day,
Elijah drank from it, and each day,
God sent birds with food.
Elijah stayed there until the brook dried up.

Elijah Helps a Widow

1 Kings 17:8–16

God told Elijah to go to a nearby town.
There he would find a woman who would
take care of him. When Elijah arrived,
he saw a widow gathering sticks.
He asked her for some water and bread.

The woman said, "My son and I
only have enough flour and oil
for one last meal."
Elijah replied, "Don't be afraid.
God will not let you go hungry."

The woman poured him some water
and made him some bread.
Because she took care of Elijah, God
took care of her. The woman's flour
and oil never ran out!

Fire From Heaven

1 Kings 18

Ahab was still king of Israel. He prayed
to an idol called Baal. He asked Baal
to bring rain, but rain did not fall.
The crops did not grow.
The people cried, "We are hungry!"

The prophet Elijah brought King Ahab
a message from God. Elijah said,
"There is no rain because you worship
a statue instead of the true God!"
This made King Ahab very angry.

Elijah wanted to show the people that
his God was the one true God.
So Elijah gave them a challenge.
He and King Ahab and all the
Israelites marched up Mount Carmel.

Elijah told the worshipers of Baal,
"Build an *altar* for *your* god.
I will build an altar for *my* God."
Then they placed an offering on each altar.

The worshipers of Baal cried out
for their god to send fire. They danced
around the altar, but nothing happened.
Elijah teased Baal's priests,
"Maybe Baal is on vacation!"

Elijah dug a trench all around his altar.
He poured water over everything. Water
even filled the trench. Elijah prayed.
Suddenly fire came down from heaven.
The *sacrifice* burned up.
The stone altar burned up.
Even the water in the trench was gone!

When the people saw what had happened,
they bowed down and worshiped
the one true God. Before long,
God allowed it to rain again.

Chariot of Fire

1 Kings 19:19–21; 2 Kings 2:1–13

A man named Elisha was plowing
the field. God chose Elisha to be
Elijah's helper.

Over the years, they traveled together.
They told many people about God's love.

One day, they stopped beside a river.

Elijah took off his coat and struck
the water with it. The river opened up!
They walked across on a dry path.

Elijah was getting older. God was
preparing to take him to heaven.
Elijah asked Elisha if there was
anything he wanted. Elisha answered,
"I want a double portion of the spirit
God has given you."

Suddenly a fiery chariot pulled by fiery horses came down from the sky. It separated the two of them, and Elijah went up to heaven in a whirlwind to be with God. Elijah's coat fell to the ground. Elisha picked it up. He struck the water with it, and the water parted. Then Elisha knew God had granted his request.

Jars of Oil

2 Kings 4:1–7

Elisha helped many people.
One day, he met a woman.
She was very upset. She said,
"Please help me. I owe a man
some money."

"If I do not pay him," the woman said,
"he will make my sons become his
slaves!" Elisha asked her,
"Do you own anything?"
She said, "I have a little oil."

Elisha said, "Gather some empty jars
from your friends. Then go inside
and pour your oil into them."
The woman obeyed, and God made
her tiny bit of oil fill all the jars!

She sold all the oil and paid the man back.
She took care of her family with the
leftover money.

Elisha's Room

2 Kings 4:8–17

Elisha often traveled to the town
of Shunem. He became friends
with a nice couple who lived there.

226

One evening, while Elisha was
visiting, the couple surprised him.
They said, "We built a room in our
house just for you."

227

Elisha was so thankful for his friends.
He prayed for them to be happy.
Elisha said to the woman,
"A year from now you will have a child."

Sure enough, a year later God
gave them a beautiful baby boy.

Naaman Is Healed

2 Kings 5:1–15

Naaman was a great army commander.
He was a brave soldier, but he had
a problem. He had a terrible skin
disease called *leprosy*.

One day, Naaman's wife said,
"My servant told me you should go see
the prophet Elisha. He can heal you."

Naaman reached Elisha's home.
Elisha sent out a man with this message:
"Dunk yourself in the Jordan River
seven times. Then you will be healed."

At first, Naaman thought it was a silly idea. But his servants said, "Please go. This is not a hard thing to do."
So Naaman dunked himself in the Jordan River seven times. When he was done, Naaman's skin disease was gone!

Naaman was so excited that he ran
to thank Elisha for curing him.
Naaman said, "Israel's God
is the *only* true God!"

Boy King Josiah

2 Kings 22:1–23:3

A boy named Josiah became the
king of Judah when he was
only eight years old. Josiah loved God.
Many bad kings had ruled before him.

The temple in Jerusalem had started to crumble. People had not worshiped there for many years. King Josiah decided to fix it up. He wanted his people to worship God in the temple again.

So King Josiah hired workers to repair it.
One day, as the men were working,
a priest found a scroll hidden in the wall.
The priest showed the scroll to the king.

It was the *Book of the Law*.
King Josiah called everyone together.
Then he read them God's laws.

The people all made a promise to
each other and to God:
"We will always obey God's laws."

The Brave Queen

Esther 1–10

Esther was *Jewish*. That means she was
an Israelite. She lived in the land of
Persia with her older cousin Mordecai.

The king of Persia needed a new queen. He announced, "Bring me the most beautiful women from all over my kingdom." Esther was one of the women sent to the palace. When the king met Esther, he chose her to be his queen.

Haman was the king's chief helper.
He hated the Jewish people. They were
God's people. Haman wanted everyone
to bow down to him. Mordecai refused
to bow down to Haman. Mordecai
would only bow down to God.

Haman went to the king. He said,
"The Jews are bad people. You should sign
a law that will help me get rid of them."
So the king signed the new law.
God's people were in great danger!

Mordecai heard about the new law.
He ran to tell Esther, "You must save
yourself and the rest of God's people.
Perhaps God has made you the
queen for this reason."
So Esther came up with a plan.
It would be very risky for her.

Esther invited the king and Haman to
a special dinner. Then she asked the king,
"Why does Haman want to get rid of me?"
The king was surprised. She said,
"I am Jewish. Haman tricked you into
signing a new law that would get rid
of all the Jews."

The king told his guards, "Arrest Haman!"
Then he made Mordecai his new
chief helper. He told Queen Esther,
"I will make a new law that will keep
you and your people safe."
God used Esther to save his people!

Fiery Furnace

Daniel 3

King Nebuchadnezzar's army had defeated
the Israelites. Now he was their ruler.
King Nebuchadnezzar built a golden statue.
Then he made a bad law. It said,
"When the music plays, everyone must bow
down and worship the statue.
Those who disobey will be thrown
into the fiery furnace."

The music began to play. The people
fell down and worshiped the statue. But
Shadrach, Meshach, and Abednego
refused. "We only worship the true God,"
they said. The king was mad!

The king said, "Make the furnace
extra hot!" He had the three men thrown
inside. Yet, when the king looked
into the furnace, there were four men
walking around! One of them looked
like an angel from God.

The king shouted to the men,
"Come out! Your God has saved you!"
The fire had not hurt them. They did not
even smell like smoke! So the king made
them rulers in his kingdom.

Daniel and the Lions

Daniel 6

Darius became the new king of Babylon.
Daniel was his chief helper. The king's
other helpers did not like Daniel.

They said to the king, "You are such a wonderful king. You should make a new law that for the next 30 days, everyone must pray only to you. If they disobey, they will be thrown into the lions' den."

King Darius made the new law, but
Daniel kept praying to God because
Daniel loved God. The king's helpers
caught him praying.

They told King Darius, "Now you must
throw Daniel into the lions' den."
The king knew he had been tricked,
but he had to obey his new law.

Daniel was thrown into the lions' den.
He was not afraid. He knew God would
take care of him. King Darius told Daniel,
"I hope your God will save you."
That night, the king could not sleep.
He was too worried about Daniel.

At sunrise, the king hurried to the lions'
den. "Has your God saved you from the
lions?" he called. "Yes!" answered Daniel.
"My God sent his angel to protect me."
So Daniel returned to the palace. Then
King Darius ordered everyone to honor and
respect God.

Jonah and the Big Fish

Jonah 1:1–3:10

Jonah was a prophet of God.
One day, God told Jonah,
"Go to the big city of Nineveh.
Tell them to stop doing bad things."

257

But Jonah ran away. He did not want
to go to Nineveh. Instead he got on
a boat to sail across the sea.
God sent a big storm to stop Jonah.
The sailors on the boat were afraid.
They thought the boat was going to sink!

Jonah told the sailors,
"My God has sent this storm.
If you throw me into the water,
the sea will become calm again."

So the sailors threw Jonah
into the raging sea.
Instantly, the sea became calm.

Just then, Jonah saw a big fish coming!
Gulp! The fish swallowed Jonah.

For three days and nights, Jonah was
inside the fish. He prayed to God,
"Please forgive me."

262

Then God told the fish to spit Jonah onto
dry land. God told Jonah a second time,
"Go and tell the people of Nineveh
to stop doing bad things."

This time, Jonah obeyed God.
The people in Nineveh
were sorry for doing bad things,
so God forgave them.

The New Testament

Timeless Bible Stories

An Angel Visits Mary

Luke 1:26–38

God sent the angel Gabriel to visit
a young woman. Her name was Mary.
She was scared. She had never seen
an angel before.

Gabriel said, "Don't be afraid. You are
very special to God. You will become
pregnant and give birth to a son.
You must name him Jesus.
He will be called the Son of the
Most High God."

Mary asked, "How can it be so?
I am not married."

Gabriel answered, "With God,
all things are possible."

Mary said, "I love God. I will do
what he has chosen me to do."

Baby Jesus Is Born

Luke 2:1–7

Mary loved Joseph. Mary and Joseph were
going to be married soon.
Joseph lived in Nazareth, but his
family lived in Bethlehem.

A new leader named Caesar ordered all
people to go back to their homeland.
He wanted to count all the people
in his kingdom. So Mary and Joseph
went to Bethlehem.

Mary was going to have her baby soon.
When they arrived in Bethlehem,
they looked for a safe place to sleep,
but all the inns were full.

Finally, a man was able to help them.
He said, "I do not have any rooms left,
but you are welcome to sleep
in the stable."

Joseph made a warm place for Mary
to rest. While they were there,
little baby Jesus was born.

Mary wrapped Jesus in strips of cloth
and gently laid him in a manger.

Shepherds Visit

Luke 2:8–20

On the night Jesus was born,
shepherds were watching their sheep.
Suddenly, an angel stood before them,
and God's light shined all around.

The angel said, "Do not be afraid. I bring
joyful news to all people. Today, in the
town of Bethlehem, a *Savior* has been
born! He is lying in a manger."

Then a choir of angels appeared.
They sang, "Glory to God in the highest!
Peace and goodwill to everyone on earth!"

The shepherds rushed to Bethlehem.
There they found baby Jesus.
They told Mary and Joseph
what the angel said.

As they returned to their sheep,
the shepherds told everyone what they
had seen and heard. All along the way,
the shepherds shouted praises to God.

Simeon and Anna
Meet Baby Jesus

Luke 2:25–38

Mary and Joseph took baby Jesus
to the *temple*. There they met
a godly man named Simeon.

Simeon took Jesus in his arms and praised God. He knew Jesus was the Savior of all people. Then Simeon blessed Jesus, Mary, and Joseph.

A prophet named Anna lived at the temple. She prayed to God every day.

When Anna saw baby Jesus,
she thanked God. She told everyone
in the temple, "This is God's Son,
the Savior of the world!"

The Bright Star and Three Visitors

Matthew 2:1–12

When Jesus was born, God put a special star in the sky. Some Wise Men who lived far away saw this star.
They knew it was a sign from God that a new king had been born.

The Wise Men followed the star.
On their way, they stopped in the city
of Jerusalem to see King Herod.
The Wise Men wanted to ask him
about the baby king.

Now, Herod was a mean king.
He tried to trick the Wise Men.
"You must find him for me so
I can worship him too," he said.

The star led the Wise Men to Bethlehem.
There they found little Jesus.
They worshiped him and gave him
gifts fit for a king: gold and
sweet-smelling spices.

An angel appeared to the Wise Men
in a dream. He warned them,
"Do not go back to King Herod."
So the Wise Men went home on
a different road.

An Angry King

Matthew 2:13–23

When the Wise Men did not return,
King Herod became very angry.

He yelled at his soldiers,
"Go and find the boy!
I will be the *only* king of the Jews!"

But God's angel warned Joseph
in a dream, "Take your family and
escape to Egypt. Do not return
until I tell you it is safe."

That night, Joseph and Mary left
for Egypt with baby Jesus.

Years later, God's angel said to Joseph
in a dream, "King Herod is dead.
Now, it is safe to leave Egypt."
So Joseph, Mary, and Jesus left Egypt and
went back home to Nazareth.

Jesus Is Lost!

Luke 2:41–52

Jesus grew up in Nazareth. Every year, Jesus and his family would go to Jerusalem to celebrate the *Passover* Feast.

When Jesus was twelve, they went
to the Feast as usual. The streets
were crowded with people.

On the way back home to Nazareth,
Mary and Joseph couldn't find Jesus.
They asked their relatives and friends,
"Have you seen Jesus?"
But no one knew where he was.

Mary and Joseph went back to Jerusalem.
They looked and looked for Jesus.

Finally, after three days, they found him!
Jesus was talking with the teachers
in the temple. The teachers were amazed.
Jesus was very wise for such a young boy.

Mary and Joseph rushed to Jesus. "We were so worried about you!" said Mary.

Jesus knew God was his Father. He said,
"I had to come to my Father's house."
He loved and obeyed his parents too.
So he returned home with them
and grew stronger and wiser.

John Baptizes Jesus

Matthew 3:1–17; Mark 1:1–11; Luke 3:1–22; John 1:1–34

John was born just before Jesus was. They were cousins. When John grew up, he lived in the desert and ate bugs and honey.

303

John told the people about God.
They asked him many questions about
what is right and what is wrong.
John told them to be good and
kind and honest.

John preached about God's forgiveness.
Many people decided to follow God.
John *baptized* the people in a river.

John told the people to get ready for a
special person who would save them from
their sins. One day, Jesus came to the river.
John knew Jesus was that special person.
Jesus told him, "I need to be baptized
by you." John was surprised, but Jesus said,
"It is right for you to do this."

So John took Jesus into the Jordan River
and baptized him. The *Holy Spirit* came
down from heaven in the form of a dove.
It landed on Jesus. Jesus smiled.
Then God said, "This is my Son, and
I love him. I am very pleased with him."

Jesus Chooses His Disciples

Matthew 4:18–22; 9:9; 10:1–4; Mark 1–3; Luke 5–6

Jesus began to tell people about God.
He knew he had a lot of work to do,
and he went to find some helpers.

As Jesus was walking along the seashore,
he saw some fishermen.
Jesus called to them, "Come. Follow me.
I will make you fishers of *people*."

Right away, they left their boats
and followed Jesus. Their names were
Peter, Andrew, James, and John.

Later, Jesus met a tax collector named
Matthew. His job was to get the tax money
from the people and give it to the king.
Matthew quit his job to follow Jesus too.

Jesus chose some more people.
Their names were Philip, Bartholomew,
Thomas, and another man named James.

JOHN

JAMES
SON OF ZEBEDEE

PETER

MATTHEW

ANDREW

Thaddaeus, Simon, and Judas joined them
too. Jesus now had twelve new followers.
He called them his *disciples*.
Jesus taught them about God's love.

Jesus' First Miracle

John 2:1–11

Jesus went to a wedding with his mother
Mary and his disciples.

Mary heard the servants say,
"There is no more wine.
What can we do?"
Mary told the servants,
"Do what Jesus tells you to do."

Jesus said, "Fill up six jars of water.
Dip out a cup and give it to your master."

When they did, they saw wine instead
of water! The servants were amazed.
When their master tasted the wine,
he told the groom, "You have saved
the very best wine for last!"
The disciples were also amazed.
This was Jesus' first *miracle*.

Jesus Teaches on a Mountain

Matthew 5:1–12; 6:25–34; Luke 6:17–23; 12:22–31

All sorts of people went to see Jesus.
Children, mothers, fathers,
grandmas, and grandpas.
They all wanted to hear what
he was teaching.

318

"Look at the birds," said Jesus.
"Do they store up food in a barn?
No. God feeds them."

"Look at the flowers," said Jesus.
"They don't work or make clothes.
God dresses them in lush leaves
and pretty petals."

Then Jesus said, "You are much more
important than birds. You are much
more important than flowers.
So do not worry. If God takes care
of them, God will take care of you."

The Lord's Prayer

Matthew 6:9–13; Luke 11:1–4 (NIV)

When Jesus was on the mountain,
he taught the people how to pray.
Jesus said,
"Our Father in heaven,
hallowed be your name,
your kingdom come,
your will be done
on earth as it is in heaven.
Give us today our daily bread.
Forgive us our debts,
as we also have forgiven our debtors.
And lead us not into temptation,
but deliver us from the evil one."

Amen.

A Captain's Faith

Matthew 8:5–13

Jesus came down the mountain
to a nearby city.
Crowds of people gathered to see him.

An army captain said, "Lord Jesus,
my servant is very sick. Please,
will you help him?" Jesus said,
"I will go to your house and heal him."

The captain replied, "You do not need to go to my house. Just say the word and my servant will be healed."

Jesus was amazed. "I have not found
anyone whose *faith* is so strong," he said.
Then Jesus said to the captain, "Go!
Your servant is healed."
The captain ran home. He was happy
to see his servant well again!

A Hole in the Roof

Matthew 9:1–8; Mark 2:1–12; Luke 5:17–26

Jesus was at a house preaching.
Many people gathered there because
they heard he was healing the sick.

The house was overflowing with people.
Many had to stand outside. There was no
room left, not even outside the door.

Down the road lived a man who
could not walk. He was paralyzed.
His friends believed Jesus could heal him.

They carried him to the house.
It was still too crowded.
So they carried him up to the roof.

The man's friends made a hole and
lowered him down to Jesus.
Jesus saw that the men had faith.
He knew how much they loved
their friend.

Jesus said to the man,
"Your sins are forgiven."
The man stood up and walked!
The crowd praised God.

Jesus Calms the Storm

Matthew 8:23–27

Jesus and his disciples got into a boat.
They wanted to cross the sea.

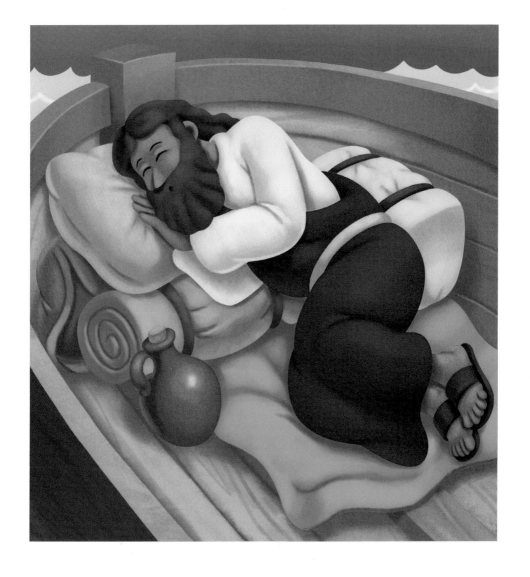

Jesus took a nap.
The waves gently rocked
the boat back and forth.

Suddenly a great storm came up.
Waves splashed over the boat.
Winds whipped around the disciples.

They woke Jesus up and shouted,
"The boat is sinking! Don't you care?"

Jesus asked, "Why are you so afraid?
Don't you have any faith at all?"
Then Jesus told the storm to stop.
Right away it was calm.

The disciples were amazed. They said
to each other, "Who is this man Jesus?
Even the wind and the waves obey him!"

Two Miracles

Matthew 9:18–26; Mark 5:21–43; Luke 8:40–56

One day, a man named Jairus came to see Jesus. He cried, "Jesus! Please come heal my daughter. She is dying."

"If you would just touch my daughter,"
Jairus said, "she would be healed." So
Jesus and his disciples went with Jairus.

A large crowd followed Jesus
as he walked to Jairus' house.

Just then, a woman pushed through
the crowd toward Jesus. She had been
sick for twelve years. The doctors
could not heal her.

The woman believed that Jesus could heal her. She thought, *I know if I just touch his clothes, I will be healed.*

As the woman got closer to Jesus,
she reached out and touched him.
She was healed at that moment!
Jesus stopped and turned around.

"Who touched me?" Jesus asked.
"I felt power go out of me."
The woman knelt before Jesus and said,
"I am the one who touched you."
Jesus said, "Your faith has made
you well. Go in peace."

Finally Jesus arrived at Jairus' house.
The people said it was too late.
His daughter had already died.

Jesus said, "Jairus, trust me.
Your daughter is not dead.
She is sleeping."

Jesus told everyone to leave the house.
Then Jairus and his wife went with Jesus
into the girl's bedroom. Jesus knelt down
beside her and said, "Wake up, my child."

Right away she opened her eyes and
climbed out of bed! Jairus and his wife
were overcome with joy.

A Fishermen's Net

Matthew 13:47–49

Jesus told a story. "One day," he said,
"some fishermen took their boat out."

"They threw their net into the water.
All kinds of fish swam in the lake."

"When the fishermen returned to shore,
they dragged their net out of the water
and looked through their catch," said Jesus.

"They kept all the good fish and tossed out all the bad fish." Jesus said, "The fishermen's net is like God's kingdom."

"Everyone wants to be part of his kingdom.
But the angels will come and separate the
godly people from the ungodly people."

"The godly people will live in heaven
with me forever."

Jesus Feeds Thousands

Matthew 14:13–22; Mark 6:30–44; Luke 9:10–17; John 6:1–15

Jesus and his disciples were tired.
They needed a quiet place to rest.
So they got into a boat and pushed off
from shore. A crowd followed the boat.

Over 5,000 people had come to see Jesus.
Even though he was tired,
Jesus wanted to help them. He
climbed out of the boat, and he
began to bless and heal many people.

Later that day, the disciples said to Jesus, "It is getting late. These people should go home and eat dinner."

Jesus replied, "We can feed them.
See if anyone has any food to share."

The disciples found one boy. He had
five loaves of bread and two small fish.
Jesus said, "Bring the boy to me."

The disciples asked, "How will so little
food feed this many people?"
Jesus said, "You will see. Have the
people sit down." Then Jesus took
the bread and gave thanks to God.

His disciples gave bread and fish
to everyone. To their surprise,
twelve baskets were left over!

Jesus Walks on Water

Matthew 14:22–33; Mark 6:45–51; John 6:15–20

Jesus told his disciples to go
on ahead of him.

Then Jesus walked up a mountainside
to pray. Storm clouds filled the sky.
Jesus could see the disciples in the boat.
They were having trouble.

The wind swooshed. The waves sloshed.
The boat was tossed about.

Suddenly, the disciples saw someone
walking on the water toward them.
They thought it was a ghost!

Jesus called out to them,
"It is I. Do not be afraid!"
The disciples still weren't sure.
Peter said, "If you really are Jesus,
let me walk out to you."
Jesus replied, "Come!"

Peter stepped out of the boat. He began
walking on the water toward Jesus. Then
Peter looked at the wind and the waves.
He became afraid. Suddenly he started
to sink. "Lord, save me!" Peter cried out.
Jesus reached out and pulled Peter up.

"Why didn't you trust me?" Jesus asked
Peter. They climbed into the boat and
the storm stopped. The disciples
worshiped Jesus. They said,
"Truly you are the son of God!"

Jesus Heals a Blind Beggar

John 9:1–12

Jesus and his disciples saw a blind beggar.
He had been blind since he was born.
The disciples asked Jesus, "Teacher,
did this man sin? Or did his parents?
Is that why he is blind?"

"No one sinned," said Jesus. "This
happened so that God's work could be
shown in his life." Then Jesus spit on
the ground and made mud out of it
with his hands. He gently spread
the mud on the blind man's eyes.

Then Jesus told the man,
"Go to the Pool of Siloam
and wash off the mud."

As soon as the mud was washed off, the
man could see! Everyone was amazed.
They wanted to find out more about Jesus.

Money in a Fish

Matthew 17:24–27

It was time to pay the temple tax.
This money was used to fix up the temple.

One day, some tax collectors said to Peter,
"Jesus does not pay the temple tax, does
he?" Peter replied, "Of course he does."

Before Peter could ask Jesus what to do,
Jesus told him, "Even though I am the
Son of God, I will pay the tax. Go fishing.
Take the first fish you catch. Look in its
mouth and you will find a coin.
Take it and give it to the tax collectors.
It will pay my tax and yours."

Peter caught a fish. He opened its
mouth and found a coin inside!
It was exactly enough to pay
the tax collectors.

The Good Samaritan

Luke 10:25–37

One day, a lawyer put Jesus to the test.
He said, "I know the law says to love God
with all my heart and to love my neighbor
as myself. But who is my neighbor?"

379

Jesus told him this parable:
"A man was on his way to the city
of Jericho. Some robbers beat him.
They stole everything he had."

"The man was hurt. He needed help. Along
came a priest. The priest saw the man, but
he did not stop. Along came a helper in the
temple. He saw the man but did not stop.
Along came a Samaritan man. When he saw
the hurt man, he stopped. The Samaritan
man cleaned up the man's wounds."

"He lifted the man onto his own donkey and took him down the road to an inn. They stayed at the inn. The Samaritan man took care of the hurt man all night long," said Jesus.

"In the morning, the Samaritan man gave the innkeeper two silver coins and said, 'Take good care of him until I return.'"

After Jesus finished the story, he asked,
"Which one of the three men was the
neighbor?" The lawyer answered,
"The one who took care of the hurt man."
Jesus said, "Go and do as he did."

Mary and Martha

Luke 10:38–42

Mary, Martha, and their brother
Lazarus were friends with Jesus.

One day, Jesus came over to visit.
Mary sat at his feet and listened
to him for a long time.

Meanwhile, Martha was busy cooking and cleaning. There was so much to do!

The longer Mary listened to Jesus,
the madder Martha got. She said,
"I am busy in the kitchen while
Mary is doing nothing!"

"Jesus, please tell my sister to help me," Martha whined.

"Martha, Martha," said Jesus,
"You should not be upset.
Mary has chosen what is better.
She is listening to me."

The Lost Sheep

Matthew 18:10–14; Luke 15:3–7

Some people wondered who was most important to God. So Jesus told them a parable.

"Think about a shepherd. What does
he do? He watches over his sheep.
He gives them plenty of food, and
he gives them plenty of water."

"He counts them up to make sure
they are all there. If one is lost,
he looks for it. He looks in the barn.
He looks near the stream. He looks
in the hills. He looks everywhere."

"The shepherd does not give up.
At last, he finds the little lost sheep!"

"He carries the sheep back.
He calls his friends together
and says, 'Let's celebrate!
My lost sheep has been found!'"

Then Jesus said, "God loves every one of his children like a shepherd loves his sheep. When one of them sins, it is like a sheep that has gone astray, and God is very sad. But when the person turns away from sin and comes back to God, he is very, very happy. He celebrates like a shepherd who has found his lost sheep."

The Lost Son

Luke 15:11–32

Jesus told another parable about God's love. "There was a man who had two sons," said Jesus. "He owned a big farm."

397

"His youngest son did not want to
work anymore. He wanted to travel
and have fun. So he asked his father
for his share of the family money."

"The son got the money. He packed his things and left. He couldn't wait to see the world! His family was sad to see him go."

"At first he had fun spending the money.
He bought expensive clothes,
and he ate fancy food.
But soon all the money was gone."

"He had to go to work and he got a job
with a pig farmer. He was so hungry that
even the pigs' food looked good.
The son wanted to go back home.
He said, 'I will tell my father
I am sorry for what I have done.
I do not deserve to be called his son.
Maybe he will let me work for him.'"

"The father saw his son coming
down the road. His eyes filled
with tears as he ran to greet him."

"The son said, 'Please forgive me, Dad.'
That night, they had a big party.
The father exclaimed, 'My son
was lost, but now he's found.'"

Jesus explained his story.
"God is like this father. He is full
of love and joy when people who
are lost come back to him."

Ten Lepers

Luke 17:11–19

As Jesus was traveling, he met ten lepers.
Their bodies were covered with sores.
The lepers shouted,
"Jesus, please heal us!"

Jesus said, "Go. Show yourselves
to the priests." The ten lepers left.
While they were walking away,
something amazing happened.

All ten of them were healed! Only
one man went back to thank Jesus.

He threw himself at Jesus' feet
and said, "Thank you!"
Jesus wondered where the other
men were. They did not come
back to thank him.

Jesus and the Children

Matthew 19:13–15; Mark 10:13–16; Luke 18:15–17

The children loved to spend time
with Jesus.

But the disciples didn't understand.
They said, "Stop. Do not bother Jesus.
He is just too busy."

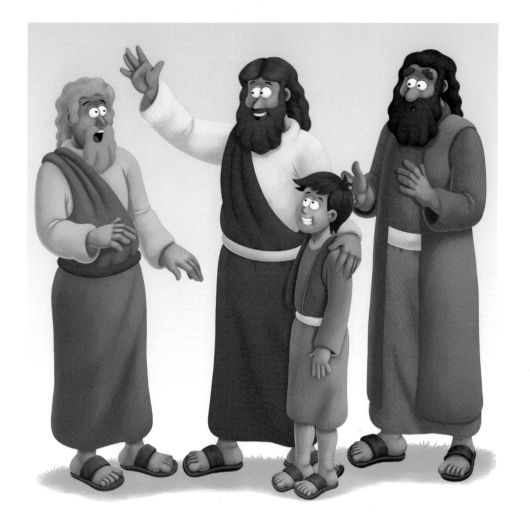

Jesus told the disciples, "Let the children
come to me. Do not keep them away.
You must become like these little children
if you want to enter God's kingdom."

Then Jesus blessed the children.

A Short Man

Luke 19:1–10

People crowded the streets to see Jesus.
Zacchaeus wanted to see too,
but he was too short.
So he climbed up a tree.

413

As Jesus was passing by, he looked up
and said, "Zacchaeus, come down.
I want to go to your house."
Zacchaeus scrambled down the tree.

Zaccheus was a tax collector. His job was to get the tax money from the people and give it to the king. Nobody liked him. He was surprised but happy that Jesus wanted to come to *his* house!

A crowd of people stood outside
the house. They grumbled,
"Why is Jesus in *there*?"

Zacchaeus told Jesus, "I will give money
to the poor. And I will pay back anyone
I have cheated. In fact, I will give them
back more money than I took."
Jesus was happy that Zacchaeus
was going to make things right.

Lazarus Lives Again

John 11:1–44

One day, Jesus received a message
from Mary and Martha.
"Jesus, please come quickly.
Lazarus is very sick." But Jesus stayed
where he was for two more days.

Then Jesus traveled to the place
where Mary and Martha lived.
Martha went to meet him.
She was crying.

Martha said to Jesus, "My dear brother
has died. If you had been here,
you could have healed him."
Jesus was sad. He cried too.

Then Jesus walked over to Lazarus' tomb.
He told some men to roll away the stone.
Jesus prayed out loud, "Father, I know you
always hear me. Now, show everyone that
you have sent me."

Then Jesus shouted, "Lazarus, come out!"
Lazarus walked out of the tomb. He was
alive again! Everyone was amazed.
Many people believed in Jesus that day.

A Gift for Jesus

John 12:1–8

One evening, Jesus and his disciples were visiting Mary, Martha, and Lazarus.

Mary poured some expensive perfume
on Jesus' feet. Then she dried his feet
with her hair.

Judas was one of the disciples. He said,
"That perfume cost a lot of money.
Mary should have sold it and given
the money to the poor."

Jesus knew the truth—that Judas wanted
the money for himself. Jesus replied, "Mary
did what is right. She honored me. You will
always have the poor among you.
But you won't always have me here."

The True King

Matthew 21:1–11; Mark 11:1–11; Luke 19:29–42; John 12:12–19

Jesus and his disciples went to Jerusalem
for the Passover Feast. Jesus told
two disciples to bring him a donkey.
He told them where to find it.

Jesus rode the donkey to Jerusalem.

A big crowd welcomed him.

People waved palm branches and put them
on the road in front of Jesus.

They shouted, "Hosanna! Hosanna!
Blessed is the king of Israel!"

The leaders in Jerusalem did not like Jesus. They saw how many people were following him, and they were angry about it. They were jealous.

432

A Poor Widow's Gift

Mark 12:41–44; Luke 21:1–4

Jesus and the disciples went to the temple area. They watched people drop money into the *offering* box.

433

The rich people put a lot of money
into the box.

Then Jesus saw a poor *widow*.
She put two small coins into the box.
"This woman's gift is greater than
all the others," Jesus whispered to
his disciples.

"Even though the woman is poor,
she gave *all* the money she had.
The rich people gave a lot of money,
but they still have plenty left over."

Washing the Disciples' Feet

John 13:3–30

Jesus and his disciples gathered together for a special Passover meal. Jesus knew he would be leaving them soon.

437

After supper, Jesus removed his outer
clothing. He wrapped a towel around
his waist. Then he filled a bowl with
water. Jesus washed and dried the
disciples' feet, one by one.

Then it was Peter's turn. He said to Jesus,
"Lord, you should never wash my feet."
Jesus answered, "I *must* wash your feet
for you to be part of my kingdom." Then
he said to them all, "As I have washed
your feet, you must wash each other's
feet." By doing this, Jesus showed his
friends how to love and serve each other.

Jesus told them, "One of you will
turn against me tonight."
His disciples were shocked and said,
"We would *never* do that!"

"Who will turn against you?" John asked.
"The one I give this piece of bread to,"
said Jesus. He handed it to Judas and said,
"Do what you must." Judas quickly left.

The Last Supper

Matthew 26:17–29; Mark 14:12–25; Luke 22:7–19; John 13–14

Then Jesus did something else.

He picked up a loaf of bread and blessed it.

Then he broke it into pieces.

He gave the bread to his disciples to eat.

Jesus said, "This bread is my body.

Every time you do this, think of me."

In the same way, he took a cup of wine
and blessed it. He gave it to the disciples
to drink. "This is my blood. It is poured
out to forgive the sins of many."

"The time has come for me to go away.
Where I am going, you cannot go yet.
I am going to *heaven* to prepare a
wonderful new home for you.
But I will return to you soon."

"At first, you will be very sad.
But do not be frightened.
Soon you will understand
and you will be filled with joy."

Jesus Is Arrested and Crucified

Matthew 26–27; Mark 14–15; Luke 22–23; John 18–19

Judas went to the leaders. He asked, "How much will you pay me if I help you capture Jesus?" They said, "Thirty pieces of silver." So Judas took the money and made a plan.

Jesus had gone to his favorite garden
to pray. The disciples went along.
Jesus prayed, "Father, if it is your will,
I am ready to give my life so that
all the people who trust in me will be
saved from their sins."

Soon, Judas arrived with some soldiers.
Peter wanted to protect Jesus.
But Jesus said, "No. I must allow this
to happen." All the disciples ran away,
and the soldiers arrested Jesus.

They took Jesus to the leaders.
The leaders said, "You say that
you are the Son of God.
We do not believe you."

The soldiers took charge of Jesus.
They made him carry a big wooden cross.
They took him to a place called
The Skull (*Golgotha*).
There they nailed Jesus to the cross.

Jesus died on the cross.

Everyone who loved Jesus was very sad.
But they forgot something important. Jesus
had said he would see them again soon!

Jesus Is Risen!

Matthew 28:1–10; Mark 16:1–10; Luke 24:1–11; John 20:1–18

After Jesus died, some of his
friends laid his body in a big tomb.
They sealed it shut with a large round
stone. Soldiers guarded the tomb.

Three days later, the earth shook. An angel
of the Lord came down from heaven and
pushed the stone away from the tomb.
Then the angel sat on the stone.

When the soldiers saw the angel,
they fell to the ground.

Mary was walking to the tomb with some
of her friends. They saw the angel, who
said, "Do not be afraid. Jesus is not here.
He has risen!"

"Go and tell Peter and the other disciples that Jesus is alive!"

On their way, the women saw Jesus.
They fell to their knees and worshiped
him. Jesus smiled and said, "Go tell the
others that I will see them in Galilee."
So Mary ran to tell the disciples.

Jesus Returns

John 20:19–20

The disciples had locked themselves in a small room because they were afraid the leaders would send soldiers to arrest them.

459

Suddenly, Jesus appeared to them!
He said, "Peace be with you."
They thought he was a ghost. But Jesus
said, "Touch my hands and my feet
so that you will know it is really me."

The disciples cheered! They were
very, very happy to see Jesus again.

A Net Full of Fish

John 21:1–14

Peter went fishing with some of the
disciples. They fished from their
boat all night, but they did not
even catch one fish.

462

Early the next morning, someone from the shore shouted, "You have not caught any fish, have you?"

"No," they replied. "Cast your net to the right side of the boat," the man said.

As soon as they did, their net was
full of fish! Then Peter knew the man
was Jesus. He jumped out of the boat
and swam to shore.

Jesus asked him, "Do you love me?"
Peter said, "You know I do."
Jesus said, "If you love me, then
take good care of my people."

Jesus Goes to Heaven

Matthew 28:16–20, Luke 24:44–51; Acts 1:6–11

Jesus had told his disciples, "I gave my life so that you could be with me in heaven. I am going there to prepare a wonderful new home for you. When I come back the next time, I will take you with me."
But now it was time for Jesus to leave.

Jesus said, "God has given me
complete power over heaven and earth.
Go and tell everyone the good news.
Make new disciples. Baptize them and
teach them to obey my commandments.
Don't ever forget, I will always be
with you."

"Go to Jerusalem and wait there,"
said Jesus. "The Holy Spirit will come to
you. He will give you power to tell people
about me. Now the time has come for me
to go to heaven. Do not be afraid."

Then Jesus went up toward heaven
in a cloud. His disciples stared at the
sky for a long time.

All of a sudden, two angels appeared.
They asked, "Why are you standing here
looking at the sky? Jesus will return the
same way you saw him go."

Then the disciples remembered what Jesus had said. They returned to Jerusalem and waited for the Holy Spirit to come.

The Holy Spirit Comes

Acts 2

Thousands of people went to Jerusalem to celebrate a Jewish holiday called *Pentecost*. They came from many countries and spoke many different languages. Jesus' disciples were staying there. They were praying together.

Suddenly, a noise filled the room.
It sounded like a strong wind blowing.
The *Holy Spirit* appeared as
tongues of fire on each of them.

They started talking in languages
they did not know.
The people in Jerusalem heard the noise
and came to see what was happening.

The crowd was amazed and asked,
"How are you able to speak *our*
languages?" Peter said, "The prophets
told us this would happen."

Then Peter told them about God's plan.
"God sent Jesus to save everyone
from the bad things we have done."

The people asked, "What should we do?"
Peter replied, "Ask Jesus to forgive you
for your sins and be baptized in the
name of Jesus Christ."

On that day, 3,000 people believed in
Jesus. The disciples baptized all of them.

The First Church

Acts 2:42–47

The new believers studied with
the disciples. They learned many things
about God and God's plans.

They prayed together.

They sang songs and praised God.

They ate meals and celebrated the Lord's
Supper together. They shared everything
they had with each other.
God added more and more believers
to the church every day.

The Lame Man

Acts 3:1–10

One day, Peter and John were going
to the temple. They saw a man
who could not walk. He had not
been able to walk his whole life.
The man was begging for money.

484

Peter told him, "We have no silver or gold.
But we will give you what we do have.
In Jesus' name, stand up and walk!"

Immediately, the man jumped up.
His legs were strong! He began
walking and leaping and praising God.

All the people who saw him were amazed.
Peter told the people, "We did not
make this man walk. Jesus did." Many
more people believed in Jesus that day.

A Changed Man

Acts 9:1–19

Saul did not like Jesus' followers. He was
on his way to put some of them in jail.

Suddenly, a bright light flashed around
him. Saul fell to the ground. A loud voice
asked, "Saul, why are you against me?"
Saul was afraid. He cried out,
"Who are you?" The voice replied,
"I am Jesus, the one you are against."

"Go to Damascus and you will be told what to do." When Saul got up, he could not see.

Some men who were traveling
with Saul led him to the city.
Jesus had also appeared to a man named
Ananias. Jesus led Ananias to Saul.

Ananias laid his hands on Saul and said,
"Jesus sent me to you. You may see
again. Be filled with the Holy Spirit."
Immediately Saul could see!
Then Ananias baptized him.

After this, God changed Saul's name
to Paul. He was a new man! Instead of
hating Jesus' followers, he loved them.
And he became a follower too.

Paul's Journeys

Acts 9:20–43

Paul traveled far and wide. He taught
everyone he met about Jesus. The new
believers were called *Christians* because
they were followers of Jesus Christ.

494

Paul traveled with different helpers.
He shared the good news with everyone
he met. He baptized many people.

During Paul's travels,
he started many churches.

Sometimes he would walk for
miles and miles.

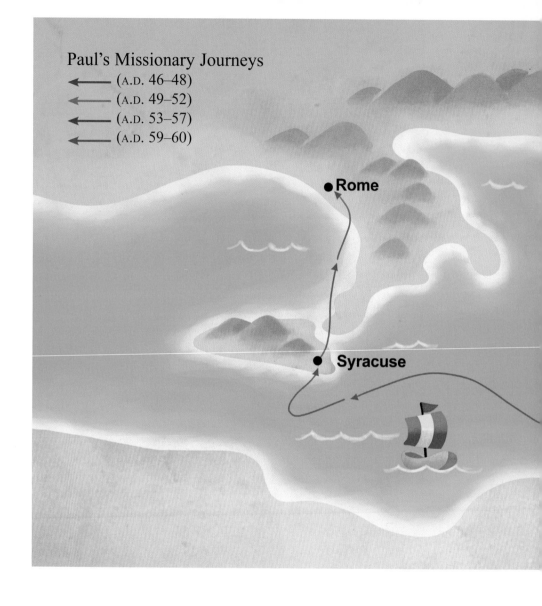

Paul's Missionary Journeys

— (A.D. 46–48)
— (A.D. 49–52)
— (A.D. 53–57)
— (A.D. 59–60)

Rome

Syracuse

Other times, he would take
a boat across the seas.

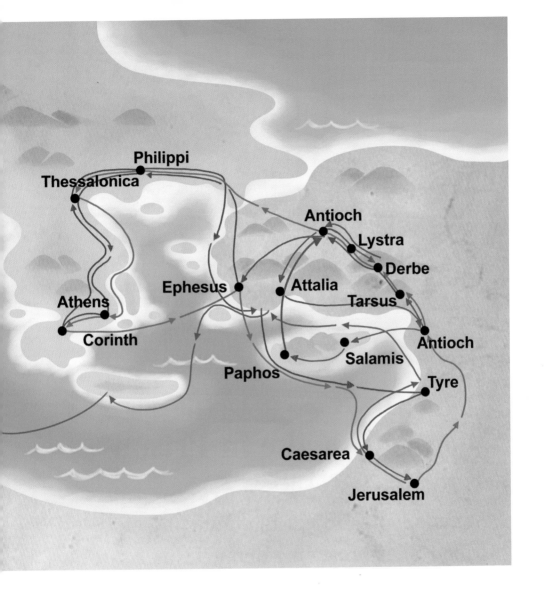

He told everyone about Jesus'
love for them.

Earthquake in Prison

Acts 16:24–34

Some people did not like Paul and his
friend Silas preaching about Jesus.
One day, they were thrown into prison.
But they were not worried. They knew
God would take care of them.

That night, God sent an earthquake.
It shook so hard that all the prison doors
opened up and all the prisoners'
chains fell off. The guard thought
everyone had escaped. He was terrified!

Paul told the guard, "Do not worry.
We are still here." The guard was amazed.
He invited the two men to his house.

The guard and his family learned
about Jesus and decided to follow him.
The next day, Paul and Silas left
to tell more people about Jesus.

Jesus Is Coming!

Revelation 1:1–2; 21:2–4

Many years later, the disciple John
lived on an island. While he was there,
an angel came to him in a vision.

In the vision, a bright light surrounded
Jesus. He spoke to John, "Do not be
afraid. Write a book about what you
see and send it to the churches."

In the vision, John saw God sitting on
his throne. A rainbow sparkled all
around him. John saw that everything
bad on the earth had come to an end.

Then John saw a new heaven and a new earth. God said, "There will be no more death or sadness or crying or pain. I will live with my people forever."

Then Jesus promised,
"I am coming back soon."

The Beginner's Bible
DICTIONARY

Some of the words in this book may be new to you. Throughout the stories you will see these words in italics. You can find out what they mean by using this dictionary.

Altar: A platform or raised place on which a gift, or sacrifice, was offered to God.

Amen: A Hebrew word that means "so be it" or "let it become true."

Anoint: 1. To pour olive oil on people or things. This sets them apart for God. 2. To pour oil on people as part of praying for their healing. 3. A sign of God's blessing or favor.

Armor: A special outer covering like clothes made of metal and leather. People wore it to help keep them safe in battle.

Army: A group of people who fight in wars.

Baptize: To sprinkle, pour on, or cover a person with water. It is a sign that the person belongs to Jesus.

Bethesda: A pool in Jerusalem where miracles sometimes happened.

Book of the Law: The first five books of the Bible; Genesis, Exodus, Leviticus, Numbers, and Deuteronomy.

Christians: People who believe Jesus has forgiven their sins and will someday live with him forever in heaven.

Commandment: A law or order that God gives.

Disciple: A person who follows a teacher. This person does what their teacher says to do.

Faith: Trust and belief in God. Knowing God is real, even though we can't see him.

Heaven: 1. The place where God lives. 2. The sky. 3. Where Christians go after they die.

Holy Spirit: God's Spirit who creates life. He helps people do God's work. He helps people to believe in Jesus, to love him, and to live like him.

Israelites: People from the nation of Israel. God's chosen people.

Jewish: Another name for a person from Israel.

Leprosy: A word used in the Bible for many different skin diseases and infections. People with leprosy during Bible times had to live in separate communities so they wouldn't infect others.

Manna: Special food sent from heaven. It tasted like wafers, or crackers, sweetened with honey. God gave it to the Israelites in the desert, after they left Egypt.

Miracle: An amazing thing that happens that only God can do. This includes such things as calming a storm or bringing someone back to life.

Offering: Something people give to God. It was and is a part of their worship.

Passover: A feast that was celebrated every year to remember the time when God set the people of Israel free from Egypt. God "passed over" their homes if they were marked with blood in the doorways.

Pentecost: 1. A Jewish celebration held 50 days after Passover. 2. The day the Holy Spirit came in a special way to live in Christians.

Priest: A man who offered gifts and prayers to God on behalf of himself or other people. He often worked in the holy tent or the temple.

Proverbs: 1. Wise sayings. 2. (cap) A book of the Bible that contains many wise sayings.

Psalms: A poem of praise, prayer, or teaching. The book of Psalms is full of these poems.

Quail: Small birds the Israelites ate when they were in the desert.

Sabbath: The seventh day of the week when the Jews rested and worshiped God.

Sacrifice: 1. To give something to God as a gift. 2. Something that is given to God as a gift of worship. See also offering.

Savior: The One who saves us from our sins. A name belonging to Jesus Christ.

Tabernacle: A traveling house of worship. When the Israelites were in the desert, their tabernacle was a tent.

Temple: The building where the Jewish people worshiped God and brought their sacrifices. God was present there in a special way.

Widow: A woman whose husband has died.

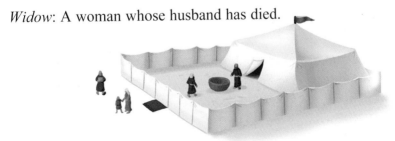

The Beginner's Bible® brand has sold more than 25 million worldwide since 1989 and continues to be a favorite for children and parents.

Visit the website **www.beginnersbible.com**. It's full of fun for kids and resources for parents and educators.